'SCAPING

Christopher Kingston

Third Leopard Press

ISBN 978-1-7365494-0-7

Cover design by: Floating Spider Entertainment

Publisher contact:
www.thirdleopard.com
info@thirdleopard.com

For my sister, Jeri, who dreamed of this day.

NOTE

    Somewhere, perhaps, there still exists someone with the leisure and the inclination to read a book of light verse. And perhaps, by some miracle, it will be this book. If so, I have a small request.

    Please read all of these poems in one sitting. It will not take long. Each poem is a riff in the album. The album is intended to be heard from the first note to the last. That the album happens to be a dead form is apropos. It's turtles — all the way.

C.K.

CONTENTS

And to 'scape stormy days, I choose an everlasting night.

JOHN DONNE

MANSCAPING

And so
      I,
living
    on
      ash
and
   antique
         time, square
my
promiscuous
mind
    upon
        plots,
hatch
   the sunlight
         in my
          egg,
wet
   my dream
        with beds,
ho ho ho
    and seed
my eye of
    green
    grown
    gold,
till
  you
    watch
and weet
in gardens
    what grow
       me.

CHRESMOI

or A Cold Day Is Hell

that never sings
        it dies.

the ultimate door,
God-made darkness —
        and the 7 things
        all clear starkness.

when hangs one whole,
        even all hale
        heathen philosophies,

your world shall neck
        where sources fail.

snakes
        fire apples.

the scattered good
shapes headless death.

experienced them feasting
        our singer-man.

breath strokes mind tall
upon His shrine and speaks:

above
are songs sung,

mid crown-fall
blazes all
in the sun,

below
white defeats
snow,

peaks —

says I,

that never sings
        it dies.

SOUTH STREET SEA PORT

per Jean Genet

A fan of the artless
the laughing seaman farts!

A loud Abbe!

Darling Prince
little years in
with his fingers of
urine scented toys.

The city!
The beer!
The boys!

The boulevard,
White Whistle
and Timbuktu.

The woman
balanced under the bridge.

Evening,
slowly leading
a subtle waltz of blood,
tosses love.

Blossomed both.

She:
as their hands meet.

He:
Divine in forbidden pockets.

Sweetly thrilling
from them
white united
flows

sailors
sweetly
them
thrilling.

WE WERE IN THE WORMHOLE

and she went to
the bathroom.

when she came
back she said,
someone wrote:

Bukowski said it right!

but not
what he said
on the wall of
the bathroom.

this is the place for us,
I said.

and then she said,
what if God's
in Heaven,
exterminator's
spray pack strapped
onto his back,
and we're crawling
under the Pearly Gates
like roaches?

this is the place for us,
I said.

we drank our
beer our backs
to the door.

BEN'S JONSON

His gut grew a belly hung over his meat
And fairly defeated the lecherous heat
That should have been fire, the sin of the glut;
His gut it did cut his hot will to a rut!

DREAM BEACH

for Nicole

I kneel before soft split spheres
of dear flesh dewed,

heaving out the head-sparking dregs
of ghostly jewels.

No blare trumpets — the bugs busy
Jew's harping the night.

No stag hunted — the racking black
moon mounting to heights

bedecked with this wilding brood
of wet stars spawned for each

Pisces-picked pebble skipping
children from dream beach.

I NEVER FELL IN LOVE SCREAMING

I never fell in love
but sat up screaming
in the dark.

In my dream
her strobing body
was a violet
the rising size
of the sun.

Laying down and
breathing hard
I reached out
across her back
and felt that she was
headless!

I screamed again.

And then a face,
pale and wide-eyed,
rose out of
the darkness
under my feet.
It said,
Jesus! What the
hell is the matter
with you?

We were both
half-asleep
two thirds terrified
and completely naked.
She was just
the wrong way
'round.

MUSIC OF THE MAIDENHAIR

(Il canto: Questo Secolo Atomico.)

Goethe, too, plucked
     the string of
          my yellow
    leaf

as now I stand
     upon a throng
          of bright notes
    beneath
         a stave
of bare
    black
        boughs.

It's worth a few bucks
    to hear my
        thrum.

The blue sky
       clear
       as a drum.

Come choir of clouds
    conducted by
        wind.

And the pale sun
    gongs
       through
    my cleft limbs.

RUN SOME THUNDER

per Charles Mingus

Charlie cello split — cleft from breast on cool feeling
bow legged and beaten by lunch bullies
and bought knives for chinking royalty

not even white enough — some brother's own father
cutely aware of d'bass't positions so high hit he
the third rail of eclecticity:

that hole in this church pours bread mingles blood
butter over my atomic rib
just don't spill your clappin' over my jam

we provide the ice and the gins in this juke
of wireless balconies fiddlin' in the Duke —
s'ain't you! so don't get lippy, ma'am

eerie pianos lay angels under rioting watts of bulb
strong arm honey hair culled from upright thighs
asks of no man but — take two

short'n'n' nothin' but pots of three month old soup
coped with carrots and sided with three gold onions
of tough black diamonds — to

empty jazz of bullshit misnomer
I pledge a whole lot of legions for the get over
and I don't want to stab you dead

                            so, Bob —

where's my motherfuckin' bread?

THE DEATH OF JUDAS

March's mirror
shocks October
into masks,
broods —

Redbrick with
goldenrod fronts
cold war
coups —

Bodhi guts
glut gullies
riven by
rain —

        blood floods the plain

TODAY

I could not make it
without murder.

I sat down unaware in
bed clothes and
ate steak and eggs
and drank dark
red wine.

I showered and shaved,
rubbed my arms and my legs
in cream and trying to dream
thought something's behind
my mind.

A rock lays hot
with a lizard on top.

This is as far as I got.

Fall's fair trove of sore leaves
under the rain.
The streaked pane.
My chin on my sleeve.

I swear
I did not cry.

Today
something important is born
but more so something
has died.

FALL

with rake
I reveal
a black-eyed
toad.

sad-eyed toad,
have the trees
let you down
too?

THIS ROPE SO HEAVY TO CLIMB

here is the vex:

it is said great poems
is
eternal.

now

eternity
is
as eternity
is

&
poetry

is real toads.

toads is eternal?

(sneeze)

well what then?

birds that gather
to anoint no king of bees?

what trees will be in decacenturies?

new nations?

sensations!

isn't toads
endangered?

isn't we all?

war?
most Christian.
forgives even
murder.

the eternal question?

which
is
?

certainty now

seems rather uncertain
then.

::

O, impudent thing!
cry clocks

who are you
to wax
unorthodox?

truth will last
a thousand years —
at least!

or two?

 bah!
eternal enough
for the likes of you!

the nerve!

laying down
these threadbare thoughts.

he has no philosophy!

poetry, he says!
it stinks, say we!

where is the harmony
of love?

where is the glorious
goddamned
sea?

I confess!

I'm
grasping
gasping
gaping
aping
gs
la weeze!

it's like my B paper
on *Ulysses*!

enough already!

I
is
quits.

if you want it
go find it.

I'll take a bottle of wine
to the sun.

::

a confused age
is no call for
confused poets,
wrote Jeffers.

believing no
miracle

save one.

BROTHER IN A BOX

per Joseph Cornell

I mirrored mom's powder box and cut a hole,
then poked thimbled pins through the velvet 'cause
my brother had a cold.

Bored Utopia made omelets to ease
subconscious parrot and I spliced the sun
with a wheel of cheese.

Sorry, Sal, I never meant to crush
the film of your dreams. Rrose said quelle
surprise and I blushed.

A naked doll through wooden curls,
like moon jail sprigs that climb
to keep women girls

keep innocent crime.

ME MISS EVE

no zeros
two alka seltzers in warm water
          smell elixic pee

hung over under
          the slag of clouds
cumminin out o'
          winter warmly:

Christmas music plays
          loud

the bar is brown, the taps chrome
          the fans spin fried fish

a fallen fork screams like a girl
a mop flops slops smelling of
          nitroglycerine

my porter of tiramisu is a
          black globe of medicine
a toast to
          toasted mio

          solo
and all my gifts
          are ghosts

the root of all singing is
          one failed accord

death is its own reward

no selves
but in things

no songs
but in silence

no zeros
but infinite —
          nothing,
          she said,
we're going to the end
of the world.

HOT CHRISTMAS

Hot Christmas sticks like gum
        to the bricks on Broughton Street
Where I catch my red ball reflection
        amidst the plastic pine run
        tight around a black lamp post.

Arsenic and strawberries,
        the fruit of the New World's
        hot holiday,
And the boats big as small cities
        float between the bright buildings.

Christ — the bells are sounding
        out their death.
Not yours — nor your abortion —
        the living corpse on credit —
        but the decorticated pound.

The street is yellow with light
        long and wet — reek
        of hot piss —
As a white horse drags a black carriage
        and three fat hicks.

THE DREAMS STUFF IS MADE OF

Not exactly a sea lion
conducting an orchestra
but life is so normal that
it's weird.

Nothing seems more likely than
nothing

and yet

a dream denies the end of
all of these distinguished things,
an end to all of this sharp
stuffing.

Napoleon as a meal,
that's really hard to swallow —
the border in pieces pours
gravy.

Coming and going is it.
It's enough to drive you mad.
Like waking up in a foreign
hotel

and everyone is speaking
English bad.

DRY HUMOR OF DEADPAN DOCTORS

they want to make you
death denier

not yours but everyone
else's as if

that grief that split the world
into life that

tear that yawned the earth into
trees of gray salt

on Jekyll Island they
want to say

no to this with some new
handbook and

pressed compounds they
want to say that

my mother was mad to
drape herself

like old flags over my father's
hollow coffin

to say that she was insane
for a few years

to say that sanity
is sanitation say

keeping the sink sponge dry
in the sun

that love is a pill waiting
to happen

as if it's any of it
at all real

they want to say progress
in this field has been

miraculous

JACKPOT

Reaping books from the yard
I gave my lady's father a basket
of spring.

I said: Don't worry about us.
Just look at all of these plums
crazy!

He said: I prefer the fall.
The trees lose all of their
money.

THE WORD FROM LEUKE

per Joan Vollmer Burroughs

—:sepia static, say
 six centuries and that
                white book
                     tells
                         me
                           out!
                       my part
                        in this?
                              just
                              some
                              smart
                           Iphigenia
                      who serves
                      : lunch
                    reeking
            meat and
      funereal
   brown
   bag boys
     tricked out to
         horripilate
                with
                  flowers.
                        his beat
                           was
                              my
                           floored
                             heart!
                           there
                        interred
                      by that
                 black blooded
           ophidian of
        ...word

IT'S A LONG WAY FROM WHISKY

a far cry from poem

pictures die too
 by the light

graphite
led a ghost in for
paper

the moon

dependable

'til it's
gone

splash!
ker-plunk!

and I'm drunk
as skunks trash
all that Cal thunk

 blast
that funk
'til the sun's unsunk

then lunk
my trunk
to bunk

hunker down

and out of blue sight

for poets
              too

and by the light

SECURITY IS DANGEROUS

per Willem deKooning

a bowl of
glimpse
paints a frozen soup

bathtubs never
get
out of their nudes

no goldfish
would
eat a Matisse

and you still
don't
any English speaks

CURI   O

per an unfinished Rauschenberg

owl

       roze

  h u
ge
out of th i   s

   gold
w
  a

      s
  t
  E

PORCH GLOBES AFTER THE STORM
(Matthew 10/16)

That delicate baubles
      such as these

should survive a storm
      whence fall great trees.

TRIPTYCH

Crucified Bacon

Pearled black scales
      roll eggs
sun bake break
      out and
                  blind
wheel mad
          for the foam.

Poppled beach of
      snack-doomed
leather plucked
      by winged
            guts —
but one
                makes it!

      Francis
      rakes it

      and doubles
      down.

A
rose
against you
mortality grows
long—whiskered
heads of scream
green teeth
shot full
of
obscene quiver of lip
just a drip of
red
a
red
a
rose
how
could
I cut
you?
A
rose
I'll
leave
you
ow—
t!

                                        Pulverize
                          to feel
                                    a dog shit
                          unprimed
                  dark
                                              music
                  of this life.

                                        Annihilate
                          despair
                              with technique —
                  enslaved
                  art
                                          greedy
          for chance!

                          Bacon
                          added

                          to turtle
                          soup.

'SCAPING

acorns blazing the sky
had it out
for me.

a cheese of gauze
clouds called
storming

sound peas of splitting
on walks spread
with flush

leavings of wet
armoring green
beetle crush.

doggéd blood
all the way
to jive

scat runs
black to the
lip and dive

'scaping
ALL
;cept least shrew.

pomes crawl-kill
say he on
haught breath

and meaning it
too:
thank balls for long death.

TOKYO ROWS

12/1/15

a dozen
shoddy boats

Korean corpses
float

along the
Japanese shore

and every autumn
more

for

northwesterly
winds drive them

to unseen
asylum.

ORTUS TROAS
an alba

Asphodel fields
      rise from the sea.

Black vultures —
      white corpses.

Nothing worse
      than the sea.

A SUNFLOWER AFTER THE STORM

finished with fireworks
the limp wet stalk of
pure kingdom
lies dead upon the walk.

flat fleshy phallus
the sun has come
too late to lift you.

so I do

and find your black head
crawling with small slugs.

not sick or delicate
        just dead.

rejoice!
you're done eating dirt!
from your hot master
you are freed!

and as for me

I'll pluck the mote
from your eye and
turn another
worm

lift another
lion

lamb another
feed.

WALKING PAST THE PASTURE TO BUY OUR LAMB

the churches are empty
        everywhere but the fields
grazed by dumb
        wet lips what
        clip
no life out of the evergiving grass

the tongue runs
        hot through the heart
        of hay
bread of no crumbs
        wine of no
miracle —

no, no accomplished cry
        stalks the yield
        that green grass
        gives up gladly

what I mean is
        these horses
        know no Easter

are no better than grass
        at eating
        God's bread

yet we are better at
        death
                than any god

Spring upon the trees
        wet yellow
        and red

green grass
        cut
        and
        shit
        it
        eats
        itself
        alive

O, eaten Earth,
        you give yourself

      to galloping cannibals!

and I

      recline upon the fence
      and think it all into time

but still

      will not witness
      when they kill
      my lamb

my dinner
my —

damn

      those horses

no
Easter

A DREAM FALLS HOT WITH WINE

I dreamed of you last night, Bukowski.

I had been drinking and reading late so
I didn't remember much this morning except
you were standing beside a dusty two door brown Pinto
at a gas station beside a hot black road lined with palm trees
under a sky of tacky tuxedo.

You wore blue jeans hung low down
and a white cotton shirt opened at the collar
and bursting over your belly.

One hand in your pocket and one on the pump
you moved your skulled lips to pull on a beedi
and surveyed your fume-stinking kingdom
from behind Spanish shades.

Looking like a good duker.
Feeling like everything is
all right.

It's coming to me now
through a bright rippling smudge
of evaporating gasoline —
you bought it somehow.

You were hanging half in half out of the Pinto
and there was a red phone cord
wrapped around your neck,
the receiver twirling over a
puddle of dark blood.

The whole scene looked as if you had just heard
that the bastards had awarded you
the Nobel Prize.

Well, that sounds good but it isn't the truth, kid.
You got your oil changed, Hank.

You're toast.

Dead as the blind wall
behind the public head
where I graffiti your ghost.

ALL THE BULLSHIT

          trust me
that debris
          that lies all around us?

take some.
          reject much.

today it is better to err
          on the side of disgust.

most of it isn't worth
          a back alley bum's waddle
                    with a pissful Miller time bottle.
                    — which is worth a lot I'll
                              tell you.

          still
once in a while
even I break through
          to it
          to you

to that thing
we call
          style.

that gossamer glimpse
          of grace

we sight it
          now and again:

lace
upon ladies

light
upon men.

A BROOKLYN BOY

per Langston Hughes

Drugs is mostly
everywhere
you go
but some spots
are hard to know.
Half of the time
you can't tell
but when you have people
run up and yell
for something
or what they got to sell
or the woman asking
and willing to do
anything
for a dollar
it's sad to see
the pain.

And you go through this
just to get home
and go through it all
again.

FLOWER POWER

just to write
       WHITE FLOWERS
is a revolution,
the solution
       to this virtual
             pollution.

white power,
       i survived,
and your coke and
       your LSD.
i did not
       go mad
       or die
       at 30.

i will stick out
       your kill o' bit
reality.

for i'm here before
       even eating,
nor fear
       to say that i hate you.

the roots,
       my boots,
       kick under
             your skirt,

where worms,
       lace hides,
crawl
       your thigh's
       dark
       dirt.

IN BEER THERE IS AN OCEAN

a sea of strange brains
          within a potion

motion in the bed
          while the Earth
                    — clowning
stands
still.

O, it's clear —
in beer
          there is an ocean

 but on the bar
only a bill
the drear junk of
          jukebox

          and
                    drowning.

BEARD UNDER GLASS
for Gary Snyder

you write like the father I never had never did
and you look like him in the same way

the whole beard under glass thing.

soiled fingers button blazer over
old blue workman's shirt
small red hairs peek the collar
quick grin sharpens pierced arrow of nose.

eyes:
>cliffs
>ponds
>birch bark.

he had that same smart flash of goofing
as when serving drinks naked at a party
he leaned over an obviously uptight woman
and all vermouth said,
>Cocktail, madam?

I laugh to remember
standing at the toilet mid-yawn
when suddenly upon the sun-white window ledge
Magpie perches to say, Here comes your soil!
before flying away.

I woke from that thinking, How real it seemed!
and somehow knew who had sent me the dream.

fresh from the sheets I leapt with you
over Cold Mountain with hot coffee
then took a shit under a bright blue sky.

thinking of the tomatoes and the eggplants
my father plumbed from his little garden
in our old Long Island yard and
how they sat just like Magpie
on my mother's kitchen sill
under curtains as yellow as all of this
porcelain daylight.

or how, in the sticky gray even,
Dad showed me the toad he
unearthed with his ho.

or, real horror of my brief youth,
how he held the
longblackhairycaterpillar
in his pink palm while I
watched it creep
leaving two or three
dark balls behind it.

what are those?
poo.
EEW!

I ran to the clean safety of my room
and his crisp laughter had my back.
he thought there was plenty of time
to make me a man.

no nature for me
but he always had it

until it had him

and I was left to face
that tough American playground
another orphan.

ah, but that was all long ago and so
I stand flushing and turn to you, Gary Snyder,
for a reminder that poems can just say who they are
the way forest burns control out of our minds
the way hills roll over if we look at them sweetly
the way old books keep making new feet for
impossible shoes for to rip wine
from the hot pile of black berries
you left behind for me,
for anybody!

for whoever might pick a long walk
over this ever widening trail.

over this way I keep losing
just to have something
to find.

plenty
of time.

BRIEFLY SHE BECOMES THE EVENING

sudden
            strokes
slowly happen

briefly
            gleams
the Star's
citrine

            reds
swell volume
yell-
            ow

interfering
blue
            blindly
claws clouds
until
            quietly
pink in the
face

briefly
            she
becomes the
evening

when
            succumbing
to the knotted
knuckles of
            sharp
black trees
the
            light
goes
            -tit-
-ani-
            -um-

the door
            flaking
like skin

a warm

          breeze
through the
screen
          closing
in all
laughing
          leaves

closing

on that
          whore
of a sun

o o

per e e

sit n'n'
mcsorley's

mustard
window of
snowshine

bright on
comings

goings

of sawdust
circling

spring
          loaded
doors

O

O
v
er
going
down
Manhattan
slowly
throwing off a fur the
perfect pink
sun
sips

Hudson River lemonade

DRINK THIS FISH

for Natalie

it was one hundred degrees
and a backyard wedding.

and the centerpieces
weren't flowers

but little bowls
of little goldfish.

by one AM
we were shooting them with whisky.

they eyeballed you
from the highball

quite shocked and
though I'm no ichthyologist

mostly dead.

religion with drunk I breezed,
drink this fish!

as my wife ran around
with her bare hands

scooping dozens of them
into one round bowl.

I said, what are you doing
with all those fish?

saving them from you!

the next morning
a lot of the fish were dead.

I said, what are you doing
with all these goldfish?

buying a tank
and feeding them.

but the tank was small
the school was large

and feeding was frenzied.

every day more fish

were floating in the gray water.

and every day my wife scooped
and flushed them.

I said, they wound up like
the ones I drank

it just took a little longer.

one day there was
one fish.

a tiny metallic torpedo
with sides blazed brave crimson.

one fish.

sole survivor
of my wife's compassion.

one fish
she named Umi.

That November we rented a house
in the Catskill mountains.

I said, what are you doing
with the fish?

taking him with us.

we drove from Queens to Woodstock
the tank splashing her ankles

the whole way.

Thanksgiving morning
Umi was dead.

I'm no zoologist but I wondered
if going up the mountain was why.

this made my wife cry.

we killed Umi!

I said, what are you going
to do?

she said, we can't just flush him.

I said, what do you want me

to do?

trudging through the snow
I threw the strongest fish in the world

off the side of the blue
and white mountain.

Umi floated freezing air
down to a stream of crackling black foil

one hundred feet below.

back inside I stoked the fire
and made dinner.

we ate in what's called
relative silence.

not long after,
we split.

full stop.

plenty of fish.

and one even made it
to the mountaintop.

ODE TO PRETENTION

O, dear, O, dark
        Pretention,

where would I me
        without you?

The Bach safari
        sounds delightful but
        what about the locals?

Wont they get vocal about
the crimes we intend to commit,
        you and I,
                Pretention?

We aren't getting too old
        to outlaw
        are we,

Pretention?

I didn't think so.

O, Pretension!
        Let's go big this time!

We know how Mother Goose
gets down, don't we,
Pretention?

        So, question:

Do you think that mama
        will really bow

to our Rabelaisian
        intentions?

SEARCHING THE AMAZON FOR POETRY

I find her lying in the bushes,
feet in the air, legs like perfect wine bottles.
Her skirt is around her neck
and her stilettos are on her hands.
Her beautiful lips are busted
and her Byronic nose bloodied.
In the distance her purse glitters
against the green undergrowth.

Extending a bruised index, she coos,
Fetch Mother's clutch, darling, and forever
        will I love you.

Panting, I hand it over and ask,
But what happened to you?

Oh, it was dreadful, my dear!
Some young woman came by
and told me that I was responsible
for every rotten thing men had ever done to her.
She said that I slept with Fascists
and nobody took me seriously anymore.
She said that I was a joke,
that I was nothing more than a punchline.
So, I beat myself up
and threw myself down here,
where ever since I've been hitting myself in the face
        with my shoes.

But you're so beautiful! I cry.
Why would you do this to yourself?

Well, you know me, dear, she smiles,
        I take everything literally.

SONG FOR AGATHOCLES

Low of birth he brought the world to its knees.
His father was a potter and his mother a tease.
But his beauty was admired by the oligarch Demas,
This boy is the incarnation of Venus!
Demas then died leaving his lover, his heir,
all of his money and his widow most fair.
Fierce in battle he won the love of men most pure —
for men love nothing so much as a warrior.
So strong, so lovely was the warrior boy
that the board of 600 felt he must be destroyed.
Said the boards and the babblers,
those awful back stabbers,
This man is too pretty. His skill is too great.
Get him out of the city before it's too late.
They banished him from Syracuse but that wasn't enough.
They hired assassins, the 600 play rough.

But our man knew their minds and foiled the plan.
Spotting a beggar he said, You! Ragged old man!
Here, take thee my clothes, and I will wear thine.
Have you ever laid eyes on a tunic so fine?
With these swank duds you're sure a good job.
You can stop all this begging, you filthy old slob.
The bum was supine and kissed our man's feet,
saying, I am not worthy of this sartorial treat.
Good day to you then, said our lovely bright lad,
it does my heart good to see you so glad.
Thus parting the beggar felt nearly divine.
Now I can finally get my hands on some wine!
But it was not to be. For in Sicily a man the clothes make.
The assassination went forward but they murdered the fake.
You killed the wrong bum, the board members wailed.
Power's no fun when you consistently fail.

Then raising an army, our man he came back.
It was only a question of when he'd attack.
So the board made a deal and welcomed him home
as long as he swore he would not take the throne.
By Ceres I swear, I'll put down the sword,
abide by the laws and show respect for the board.
But that didn't stop him from speaking his mind
and generally giving the board a bad time.
He made it his mission to fight for the poor
until the day came when he could stand it no more.

Claiming the board was plotting his end
he paid a few calls to some very dear friends.
He appealed to the army and wouldn't you know
they slaughtered the 600 and took all of their dough.
And as that day came to a dark bloody close
they turned all the women in town into hos.

That night was frightful, violent, depraved.
And the great party lasted the length of two days.
Then scorning all glory our hero stripped down.
A mufti for me, I don't want any crown.
His soldiers insisted that a man of such metal
must be their dear leader so they elected him General.
Many in town were doubtful and yet
they lauded his wisdom when he cancelled their debts.
And when Carthage attacked and shut down the port
the General returned to his favorite sport.
He would sail his fleet ships to the African shore
but feared a revolt while he was off waging war.
So to keep his good people from blowing their lids
he took as his cargo a bunch of their kids.
Then burning his ships in the African surf
he marched his great army through enemy turf.

He sacked Tunis and at the gates of Carthage he frolicked
while inside the walls the people were bitching to Moloch.
How could he let such a bloodthirsty creep
bother them here where their children did sleep?
The priests thought it best to consult with the shrine
and there they discovered the cause of this crime.
Moloch loved children, his favorite meal,
and the nobles were giving him quite a raw deal.
They sent him the poor instead of their own
and for this bad grub they would have to atone.
Moloch was waiting with knife, fork and bib
as the Lords and the Ladies served up the prime rib.
That's all that he wanted, a succulent dinner,
and now he was ready to make Carthage a winner.
Our general was beaten, stranded and stumped.
But then he remembered Ophelas, that chump!

To Cyrene he sent some men with a pitch:
Help me sack Carthage and I'll make you quite rich.
All that we take will augment your throne.
All that we want is a ship sailing home.
Ophelas was eager, bitten by greed,

and ordered his army to embark with great speed.
But the march was a hard one for the desert was hot
and by the time they reached Carthage the soldiers were shot.
Our general was gushing with friendship and praise,
Lay down all your arms and rest a few days!
Ophelas was weary and took his repast
never suspecting it would be his last.
Our hero was ruthless and murdered the dupe
then petitioned the soldiers to merge with his troops.
Their leader was fallen and they'd nowhere to go
so the Cyrenaeans decided to go with the flow.

His ranks now replenished and his spirits revived
our general set out to take some more lives.
He came upon Utica and found in the fields
three hundred workers he could use as his shields.
Bound to the engines the prisoners would die
if their kinsmen would fire on the invading tribe.
But sacking the city our man was quite peeved
when his son started whining that he wanted to leave.
The army agreed and pressed for the right
so the father, our hero, slipped out in the night.
The soldiers had had it with their general and son,
so they slaughtered the latter leaving daddy quite stunned.
Enraged, our tyrant ordered the death of all kin
of every last soldier that dared betray him.
Man, woman and child, he killed them all three
then crowned himself king of all Sicily.

Peace was rare, at home there was none,
for his wife was discovered in bed with his son.
His grandchild stabbed another to death
and here's how the king was to draw his last breath.
Menon, his servant, a Segestan by race,
was also the owner of one pretty face.
In love with his beauty, like Demas before,
our king took him captive, his slave to adore.
Now Menon, full of cunning and guile,
always attended his king with a smile.
In secret he plotted the death of his master,
the man who had made his life a disaster.
Patient he found a habit to use
to murder the man, the source of his blues.
Like Moloch reposing after a feast
the king always picked at the stuff in his teeth.

One night, when the king had called for the bill,
Menon gave to him a detritus-dipped quill.
The master, contented,sat there and hummed,
unwittingly smearing black death on his gums.
It didn't take long for the pain to begin
and his mouth to be filled with a toxic gangrene.
He assembled the people with a plan to decree
that if they avenged him they all would be free.
The people came out to hear the new laws
but the king could not move his spore-swollen jaws.
Seeing him thus, they bade him retire
by placing him living on a bright funeral pyre.
His body was writhing, hot flames all around
but because of his illness he could not make a sound.
Menon escaped and acquired great fame.
He rallied the masses and planned a campaign
of war upon Syracuse, he'd make it his own,
the kingdom that one time had conquered his home.

Agathocles, beauty, soldier and king,
this, his requiem is all mine to sing:
Surviving the trials of statecraft and war
he ruled a great city and conquered ten more.
Years of fortune and daring numbered seventy-two,
when a slave laid him low with a feather of poo.

BEGOING

Yes!
he said,
      Begoing!
Begoing eyes
Begoing body
Begoing breasts cupped snow like
      over neckline of cotton
      saggingly T drifts
           poor sad woebecame abs.
Begoing
memory flesh stretched
      over the
Begoing World
      through ice Cold
          Nothing
      burned with Stars
         Begoing
             no
      where.
While
we are Begoing Soul
      swimming
      through our own
Einskein
      of
      All
begone
      inside
         out of
            itself
      :
you
      me
         we
            they
      hey!
don't   stop
for
         Death
      say,
Hell,
      we really should
         begoing...

IN WINE I WATCHED THE DAY DISAPPEAR

a week.
a year.

a lifetime.

over and over and over
again.

my father.
my sister.
my friend.

gone.

so why worry
about a day
washed out with wine?

fingers still move.
feet still throb.
god still dies.

over and over and over
again.

and the children.
they keep coming.
keep stealing
a little more sun.

will it ever be done?

did it ever begin?

over and over
and over
again.

so I should worry?

I should pray
as darkness pierces day?

I may —
but there's a chance here.

a lance
a spear of light

from the moon.

soon.
soon.

it will shine.

it will be
all mine.

mine.
in time.

and here!

or
none of it.

for one by
one

they appear.

the stars.
the stars.
the stars.

the stars
            ruin
everything.

الربع الخالي
Koyaanisqatsi

abrading mist
of sand veils
static waves of
gray dunes
etched by the
same hot wind

your breath
over these
words

THE NEW FEW

for Henry

An open window, an empty chair,
    a forbidden prayer echoes the fallow field...

And comes to you
    Patmos 2021.

See, he has come!
    Invader, usurper,
    chain upon brain,
    wolf among the flock.

But for you alone I scribble this lock,
    and swallow it for future grok:

        5-7-12-13.

Discover where these numbers dwell
    and you will part the curtain.

Remember our deal:
    Damascus steal!
    Break the cobra's wheel.

De-dupe yourself through a cultivated lucidity.

You have the beads,
    thumb them with honest humility.

Avoid the cities
    but infiltrate regularly.

Smile, nod, laugh, play,
    when you can, agree.

Otherwise silent,
    witness, wait,

forever ready to annihilate.

There can be no mercy for the merciless.

You will know them,
    for they are legion,
    open, secure, absurd.

It is always easy to sniff the herd.

Does your patrimony groan from Elysium?
    But he still exists!

Take up the sword, trench the wine,
    lambs for the katabasis.

I have shown you the one faith,
    the practice to one strength,
    and the way of the royal art.

Not thinking but being
    a green dragon,
    a slain bull,
    a pure fire heart.

Ignis centrum terrae,
    a stallion jockeyed by God!

You know the four laws,
    you gather the five limbs,
        you conquer the seven kingdoms within.

Woman
you wed.

Man
you defeat.

Child
you berry.

The throne
is your seat.

You fear nothing.
You kneel before no one.

For I am your Gray Father,
you my Immortal Son.

And your reign be secured
if what I ask be done:

Upon the fifth place build the temple,
    erect an altar but no cross.

I give you the leopard,
    blazoned black and red embossed.

To this house other living men will fly,
    as the laughing dead crawl on by.

Evolve rites, creeds and codes,

dress in esoteric modes.

Become the new few,
    narrow the road, wide the view.

Go armed, awake and avowed,
    whisper, signal, and confound.

Be hard as gin,
    and smooth as cream,

    grin, and guard
        the wells you plumb.

    Fathomless dream, awful Day,
exquisite beast, come the way.

AGE OLD OLD AGE

I have no money
nor job
and forty —

by gob!

Soon
I'll be dead.

Easy enough.

But what of rough
seventy?

The wracking rack of
frozen bone.

Wearing my scrotal sac over
my skull.

Who will love me?

How will I get my
morphine?

The Times!

What a joke!

When even gods have been made
to crawl!

I'll just have to
worm my way out, folks.

That's all.

P. S.

I confess I confess
nothing

Those who would seek my
soul

Will find my
foot

www.ingramcontent.com/pod-product-compliance
Lightning Source LLC
Chambersburg PA
CBHW020602030426
42337CB00013B/1180